Serve me Better...
Please!

An approach to GREAT Customer Service

A Guide for Customer Service Reps and their Managers

Francesco Messina

Order this book online at www.trafford.com
or email orders@trafford.com

Most Trafford titles are also available at major online book retailers.

Note for Librarians: A cataloguing record for this book is available from Library
and Archives Canada at www.collectionscanada.ca/amicus/index-e.html

Printed in Victoria, BC, Canada.

ISBN: 9781-4269-102-9-6

*Our mission is to efficiently provide the world's finest, most comprehensive
book publishing service, enabling every author to experience success.
To find out how to publish your book, your way, and have it available
worldwide, visit us online at www.trafford.com*

Trafford rev. 9/2/2009

 www.trafford.com

North America & international
toll-free: 1 888 232 4444 (USA & Canada)
phone: 250 383 6864 ♦ fax: 812 355 4082

Contents

ACKNOWLEDGMENTS

I want to thank my parents and my sister for their constant help and support. I also wanted to acknowledge the following individuals for the help they provided in making this book possible: Stacey Mullings, Dr. Lisette McGregor DDS, and Falyne Hurst.

FOREWORD

You could probably fill an entire house with all the books ever written about Customer Service. So why am I diluting myself in believing that you would buy this one and recommend it to others? Well... Contrary to what you currently find at the bookstore, this guide is short and to the point. Do you really need to read four hundred pages of redundant babble? You are much too busy to spend that kind of time and so, to simplify your life and to exponentially increase your effectiveness, I have compressed a wealth of knowledge into less than 60 pages. Another reason you will get more mileage out of this book is that it not only presents you with easy-to-understand theories; it actually gives you concrete examples to help you put them into practice.

This book is designed to be a quick reference guide for Customer Service reps and their managers in the hopes that no one would ever have to face bad service ever again. In fact, bad Customer Service lurks everywhere. The drive-through staff putting too little or too much milk in your coffee; the courier driver who says "Oh well?!" when he delivers a damaged box; the airline employee who keeps you on hold for fifteen minutes just to hang up on you; the contractor who never comes back after doing half the work; the civil servant sending you to every single counter until you finally leave; the store clerk who seems to hide in the back room when you need help but who hovers anxiously when you don't need him... Everyone has suffered at least one of these and I say ENOUGH! I have become increasingly aware of just how bad Customer Service has become, and I think it might be due to a lack of awareness. So I am doing my part by writing this hands-on guide...

Throughout this manual, I will relay how I believe Customer Service should be dispensed and how to approach different situations. Note here that my vision is not exclusive. This means that I do not pretend to think that my way is the only way. Different people have different styles and different clients require different approaches. Reading this, you should keep an open mind and take from it what fits you and your business better. You should review the arguments presented here and discuss them with your managers and colleagues to get a broader perspective.

INTRODUCTION

WHAT IS CUSTOMER SERVICE?

You should remember that Service is an art. It is the art of making people you deal with feel you have satisfied their needs. You did it so successfully that they would prefer not dealing with anyone else and would recommend you and your company to their closest friends and family. Doing this well will not only fill you with pride and satisfaction, but it will ensure client retention and open the way to corporate expansion. In fact, managers and corporate leaders should view Customer Service as their primary marketing tool. All the billboards in the world cannot save you from clients having bad experiences with your employees, and no TV spot is greater than one of your clients telling others "call these guys, they're great!"

When you are speaking to a client you always represent your company. Whatever you say or do will reflect on your organization. Regardless if you are a service rep, a data entry clerk, a warehouse operator, or a janitor, if you get in contact with a client, you are performing Customer Service. If you are not sure what to do, find someone who does, or better yet, use the information from this guide to help you serve the client better...

GENERAL CONCEPTS

The first notion you should keep in mind is to <u>always treat a client's file, concern, or shipment, as if it was your own</u>. Their loss is your loss. Many people in the service industry are disconnected from what happens which makes them useless to their clients, their company, and to themselves. Try to imagine how you would feel if this was happening to you. The client may be losing a sale if you do not act... How would you feel if your paycheck might not come in this week unless you acted? Your stress level is probably increasing simply by reading this very first concept. But remember that this guide is not titled "Zen at work..." but "Serve me better...". I am going against the current in advocating that you personalize your work. In my opinion, this is the best way to perform Customer Service far above what is expected.

Taking it personal is important, but you must keep track of your boundaries. There are limits to how much empathy you can inject into your work. For example, if your client needs something done that would cost your company money, or if it would demand your personal involvement outside of work, or would be something un-ethical or potentially illegal, then you should stop, discuss it with your colleagues and managers, and use some of the techniques you will read about later on to explain to the client why you may not be able to resolve the situation.

Another thought that will help your success as a Customer Service Rep is to <u>act as if every call was recorded</u>. Sometimes we are tired and don't give it all we have... But if you imagine that every call you get is recorded and reviewed by your superiors, you might be more attentive.

Remembering to <u>manage your clients' expectations</u> is something that will greatly help you become a great Service provider. A SkillPath seminar I once attended called it: "Under-promise, Over-Deliver". Promise clients less than you know you can do, and deliver more than they expected. Those more "geek-inclined" then I would refer to Scotty in StarTrek and how he always padded his estimates... This is where many people fail. They promise too much, and then the client is let down, leading to arguments and dissatisfaction. Tell the client the order will be in next Friday (when you know it should be in Wednesday), then call him/her on Wednesday to advise the order is already in...

I have been lucky in this business because I am a very difficult client myself. I do not scream and complain, but I expect a tremendous level of Service from my providers, and unfortunately, I get disappointed very easily. So when I dispense Service, I always ask: "What would I expect", then I take the appropriate action. The fourth notion I therefore present suggests that you must <u>be your own worst client</u>. Think of what your most demanding client would want, and act accordingly with everyone.

If you take these four "mantras" to heart and apply them in your every day interactions using the tools mentioned throughout this guide, you will be well on your way to becoming the most rare and accomplished employee: <u>The Psychic-Rep</u>. This particular brand of Service provider is able to know what the client will need before the client is thinking about it. He/She already knows why the client is calling when seeing their name on the call-display, and is fully-prepared to answer the phone...

OVERRIDING SKILLS

Bring this book in the bathroom. Look at yourself in the mirror, take a deep breath, expand your chest, stand straight, bring your shoulders back, lift your nose slightly, look yourself sternly in the eyes and with conviction say: "I AM!". Do this again and add your name at the end of the sentence... Now say it as if you were the master of the universe... Do it twice more, or until you BELIEVE that you are the best Customer Service rep in the World.

If you sounded over the top, and if you laughed a little (or someone else hearing you made fun), then you did it right. This simple exercise serves to teach you one of the overriding skills you will need to succeed: <u>if you have confidence, you can make it</u>. Confidence is one of those attributes that you can improve through a self-help journey, but throughout this guide, you will find tools to help you gain inner strength.

Be extremely careful with confidence though. The way this exercise will make you feel could brush towards omnipotence and delusions of grandeur... But you must keep this to yourself. You may think you know all, and can do all, but you should never allude to it when speaking to others. As paradoxical as it may sound, <u>the second skill you must have is humility</u>. There is nothing worse for you than to argue with a client or vendor to preserve your ego. Let the client think they know more than you, but make "suggestions" and let them believe that the solution came from them. This will make the client feel good when they deal with you, and they will become less difficult. In my opinion your goal should not be to "break" the client into the mould you want them to follow, but instead, you should make them feel at ease and comfortable.

Example of "humility"

> ### CLIENT: You must do it THIS way!
>
> BAD Response
>
> I have been in this business for 10 years and I know it has to be done THAT way, not THIS way!
>
> BETTER Response
>
> I understand why you are suggesting THIS way. But I have noticed that many clients benefit more when I do it THAT way [explain]. [NO SARCASM PLEASE]

You are allowed to make mistakes, but you must own up to them. Of course there is a limit here. It is not because you made an error that the client can take advantage of you. This brings me to the third invaluable skill you must develop: <u>Take your mistakes and turn them into positives</u> by telling your client exactly how you intend to fix them. Hiding the error and not updating a client will be the quickest way out of your job... Also, unless you have a strong relationship with the client, evade questions about how the issue occurred. Focus instead on the resolution and what you and your company will do to avoid this in the future. Depending on the error, you may want to consult a supervisor to review the options, but YOU MUST somehow make amends. At the beginning, this will probably consist in fee reductions at the company's expense, but as you read on and with lots of practice, you will be able to compensate for most errors simply by re-assuring the client and showing that you care enough to devote yourself to fixing the problem.

Another example of "humility"

> CLIENT: You made a mistake!
>
> BAD Response
>
> No I didn't!
>
> BETTER Response
>
> I understand you're upset and let me tell you that my manager and I are working on this, and we will keep working on it until it is resolved, and I will follow up with you every hour to let you know how we are doing!

A third example of "humility"

> CLIENT: How could this happen?
>
> BAD Response
>
> Well my assistant was out for lunch, then the system deleted part of the file due to a programming error, and ...
>
> BETTER Response
>
> We are still looking into this but right now my focus is on fixing the situation... [usually, if you did a good job, the client will forget to ask again later]

Did you ever hear the phrase "the client is always right"? Well if there was a misunderstanding, it is important that you be the bigger person:

A fourth example of "humility"

CLIENT: That's not what I asked for!

BAD Response

Well that's what you said!

BETTER Response

I saw you pointing at that on the menu, then I asked if this is what you wanted. Maybe I misunderstood?

A final example of "humility"

CLIENT: That's not what you said!

BAD Response

Yes it is!

BETTER Response

I am sorry it did not come across properly. This is what I meant...

TOOLS AND TECHNIQUES

I AM SORRY .VS. I APOLOGIZE

I have heard and read that when dealing with clients, Service reps should always apologize, but never be sorry. The arguments are usually related to the fact that the employee should not personalize the contact with a customer. As you know by now, I completely disagree with this argument, but I would still advocate the use of "apologize" in certain circumstances. Here are the main differences/applications for each approach:

I AM SORRY	I APOLOGIZE
More personal	More clinical
Use to show empathy, show that you care and that you want to help	Use for general errors affecting a variety of customers
Demonstrates that the client is important	Demonstrates that the client is not the only one affected
Say "I'm sorry"	Say "We apologize"
Always explain how you will fix the problem	Always explain how/when the problem will be fixed
"I am sorry you had to wait in the rain. It appears that there was confusion with the driver but I have urgently dispatched another one to your correct address..."	"Due to high winds, several tree branches fell on electric cables and caused a general black out. We apologize for the inconvenience and service should be restored within the next few hours..."

CLARITY IS KEY

When a client has given you instructions, make sure you understand them perfectly. There is nothing worse than to quickly take instructions, do the work, then realize that this is not what the client wanted. Don't hesitate to have the client repeat, and then, repeat to the client what you have understood to make sure they agree. The same rule applies when you give information to a client. Make sure your information is clear. Clients are known to make big leaps, so frame your answers properly:

Example of "Clarity is Key"

> CLIENT: So how is my car doing? Did you finish the paint?
>
> BAD Response
>
> It's good. We just finished painting it.
>
> Next thing you know, the client will be at your door to pick up the car. So if you are not ready, he/she will not be happy...
>
> BETTER Response
>
> It's good. We just finished painting it, but we need to let it dry. The car will be ready by 8 AM tomorrow.

One thing that will help you serve better is to remember that half answered questions make half-satisfied customers. It's not enough just to be clear, you have to make sure that when you answer a client's question, they have all the tools they need to avoid further questioning. Sometimes that will mean educating them on something that will help solve their issue in the future, and sometimes it just means you should ask: "does this answer your question?"

Another example of "Clarity is Key"

CLIENT: Why are you charging me $22.00 for this call?

BAD Response

Because this was a roaming call.

BETTER Response

This was a roaming call. You were in a location not serviced by us so in these cases we have to use another company's network to make sure your call gets through. To see if you are roaming, you can look for a little "R" to appear on your phone. That's how you know you are out of our regular service area. All the calls you make then, will be more expensive. Does this answer your question?

WHAT'S YOUR NAME?

People in general like hearing others say their name. It makes them feel important and shows them you remember... Do not hesitate to use your contact's name at least once, but do not go to extremes...

Example of "What's your Name"

BAD
Hello John! How are you John? What can I do for you John?
BETTER
Hello John! How are you today? What can I do for you?

HOW TO SAY NO

You will not be able to please everyone all the time. There will be occasions when you cannot provide the client something he/she needs. When this happens, <u>never say the word "NO"</u>. Explain the situation, and provide alternatives. Empathize with your contact and show that your answer hurts you as much as it does them, or better, show that your answer is in their best interest.

Example of "How to say NO"

<u>CLIENT: Call the people overseas and get the information!</u>

BAD Response

No. That's not my job... You call them!

BETTER Response

Usually, my clients prefer to call the people overseas directly. They already have contacts there and that will not only ensure a quicker response, but you can also make sure there is no misunderstanding and therefore avoid further issues!

Another example of "How to say NO"

> <u>CLIENT: I want this dress in a size 9!</u>
>
> BAD Response
>
> I don't have it anymore. Come another time, maybe we'll have it.
>
> BETTER Response
>
> Unfortunately we already sold our last one. But let me see if one of our other locations has it. If not, I know we should be re-stocked on Monday. If you give me your contact information I can make sure we call you as soon as we get one.

A third example of "How to say NO"

> <u>CLIENT: How can you let Customs delay my shipment so much?</u>
>
> BAD Response
>
> Well that's always a risk when you do this type of business...
>
> BETTER Response
>
> Unfortunately this is left at their discretion. I will make some calls and see how long this could take, but I suggest we don't push too much or that might delay the shipment even more. I understand how this is affecting your business, and as soon as Customs does their work, I will alert you.

There are also times when the client may ask you to do things that are out of your range, something you simply do not do. In those instances, it is important to explain that this is something you do not do, and suggest where they should go for the service.

A final example of "How to say NO"

CLIENT: Give my car a good wash, will you!

BAD Response

We are a repair shop, not a car wash. We don't do that here.

BETTER Response

We are a repair shop and unfortunately we do not have the equipment to wash your car the way it should be washed. But there is a place two blocks down that does great work. I think you'll be satisfied with what they'll do for you.

YOUR MOTHER WAS RIGHT... SAY PLEASE AND THANK YOU

This is one of the simplest things you have to do, and one that is often forgotten. There is nothing scientific about saying please when asking for information, and saying thank you when receiving it... I also encourage you to say thank you before hanging up the phone or leaving a client. Even if you have helped them and they should be thanking YOU, leaving them with one of your own is always good etiquette. Be careful here though. The point of the last thank you is to show your appreciation with the fact that they came to you, or your company. I would strongly caution you against actually saying "Thank you for calling Widget Inc.". Statements like that are impersonal and often annoying to the person having to listen to it. A simple thank you is enough. If you are ever challenged (client asks why are you thanking them since you are the one who helped them), then you can expand and say "I want to thank you for allowing me to help you".

SAVE, THEN PREACH

Many times you will want to educate the client about a particular topic. They will do something rash or last minute which will cause them, and you, stomach pains and eye twitches. When this happens, many people will take the opportunity to "teach the client a lesson".

-I have told you not to do this before specifically because this would happen...!

Statements like this are poison to your relationship when injected in the middle of a crisis. First, help the client resolve the problem. Once the issue is resolved (positive or negative) that is when you preach good behaviour to the client...

-You know what happened yesterday? Let's talk about how we can prevent it in the future!

An example of "Save then Preach"

CLIENT: The wedding is tomorrow... I really need this dress here TODAY!

BAD Response

I keep telling you not to leave things to the last minute... See what happens...?

BETTER Response

Let me make a couple of call to see what I can do...[work as hard as you can to get this done]

[A few days later]- Hello. I am happy we were able to get the dress to you but we have to discuss how we can prevent this type of emergency in the future...

Another example of "Save then Preach"

CLIENT: My car is not starting and I have a really important meeting this morning!

BAD Response

I keep telling you to come in for maintenance... See what happens...?

BETTER Response

I'll send someone to boost your car right away, but you and I will have to set-up a maintenance plan later to prevent this from happening again...

OPEN YOUR EYES AND EARS

This is a skill that will take some time to achieve. While focusing your attention on what you are doing, <u>always keep one ear floating</u>. What I mean is that you should always be mindful of what is happening around you. You might over-hear things that could help your client (someone two cubicles over is talking about traffic on the highway, and that might help if you are dispatching trucks to pick up freight for a client...). You may also learn more about your business and therefore become even more useful to your client and your company.

You should also <u>keep track of what is happening with a client's file, issue, or shipment</u>. If many different people (internally) must be involved, learn to befriend them and use these relationships to get what the client needs. Remember: Clients will not call them if they are not pleased... They will call you, and they will blame you. Keep your eyes on the ball and this will make clients happy.

KNOWLEDGE IS POWER

If you are confident enough, and sneaky enough, you may still provide good Service by knowing a minimum about what your company does, and how it does it. One day however, you will be discovered and you may never recover from it. To be excellent at what you do, you must <u>understand as much as possible about your company</u>.

- What services do we provide?

- How do those compare to the competition?

- What customer's needs are met or not met by our products or services?

- How does a client apply for these services, how long does it take to become active, how long does the service last?

- How can I get a client's question answered faster?

You should know the answers to all these questions (and many more). This will give you an edge. It will make you much more valuable as you will be able to help clients better, and potentially cross-sell other products. I would not expect you to be an expert on all aspects of your company. Many of the answers will come with experience, and many of the questions will be better handled by experts. This means that you must <u>develop a network of people from different departments so you can easily access knowledge</u>.

Earlier, I mentioned that you should use your contact's name in a sentence and that this makes them feel more comfortable. Similarly, <u>knowing more about them and their company will go a long way to improving Customer Service</u>. If you know that this person is usually happy on Friday and grumpy on Monday, and you need to give them bad news, then you will know when to give it to them to minimize their reaction. If you know the type of business your client does, you may also be able to provide alternatives or new services they might be interested in... Obviously, you need to know when to offer these alternatives. If a client calls you complaining about how he was mistreated by your sales staff at the store, now is not a good time to tell him about the new Mega store you are opening up... <u>You have to know when is best to fix a problem, and when is best to cross-sell</u>.

THE BUCK STOPS HERE... BUT LET ME ASK MY MANAGER...

You are a representative of the company you work for. When an issue arises, you cannot blame it, or its employees.

Example of "The buck stops here..."

CLIENT: Your driver damaged my box!
BAD Response
I am sorry about that. Our drivers are morons... I will speak to his manager.
BETTER Response
I am sorry about that. This rarely ever happens. Let me speak to the driver and his manager and see how this happened.

Another example of "The buck stops here..."

CLIENT: Your soup tastes bad!
BAD Response
I know. My boss won't let me put spices in it...
BETTER Response
Its usually very good. Maybe something was missed on this batch. Can I get you something else?

So when something bad happens, don't blame anyone. Seem surprised even if you know the issue then promise action and/or defer to your supervisor or a manager to look into the situation with you.

PRESENTATION IS KEY...

Depending on the system used by your company, you should make sure the caller knows they are at the right place when you answer the phone. Your company may be part of the greeting, but your name should definitely be there...

Example of "Presentation is Key..."

BAD
Hello?!
BETTER
Widget Inc., John speaking :)!

You should also consider your voicemail as an extension of your service. It should be professional and to the point. Do not make mention that you are unavailable... The caller is smart enough to realize that.

Another example of "Presentation is Key..."

BAD
I am not available right now, so leave a message!
BETTER
Hello, you have reached John at Widget Inc. Please leave a detailed message after the tone and I will return your call shortly.

Those of you working in retail or who interact face-to-face with the public are not excluded from this... On the contrary, presentation is most likely the primary feature of Customer Service for you. Your client is more fickle because people don't have to shop at your store... Your competition is usually right next door.

Consider yourself the greeter and facilitator. Most important, don't hide in the back and don't talk to friends or staff. Approach the client slowly (but don't sneak up on them) with a smile and make eye contact:

A third example of "Presentation is Key..."

Hello, and welcome to Widget. Can I help you find something?
CLIENT: I'm just looking!
No problem... I'm John. Just let me know if you need anything.

Don't hover too close, but close enough that you can see if the client looks in your direction for assistance.

THE SCRIPT'S THE THING

At various times you may have to give bad news or may have to review complex situations with a client. <u>Prepare scripts for yourself as a guide</u>, but never read from them. This will allow you to review possible responses and prepare for them. The scripts should have main points and important notes in case the client asks more questions. You should always make sure you include the following points:

- What is the issue?

- Why is this the case?

- How will this be resolved? What will I do to help make sure this gets resolved?

- Who does this affect, who will resolve this, and who else could be of help?

- Will there be compensation for this? Why, or why not?

- How could this have been prevented, or how to prevent this in the future? (You do not have to answer this one, but make sure you consult your manager so you know what to say if the client asks)

Take the time to review the script you have prepared, even share it with a colleague to see if they have suggestions, then make the call. You will find an example for this topic in the "Case Study" section of this manual.

PHONE ETIQUETTE

One of the common annoyances clients face, are Service reps who do not even allow the person at the other end to say a word, and place them on hold immediately. This is insulting and frustrating, especially if it turns out the client is not at the right place. Please <u>do not place a client on hold without asking if they mind holding</u>. They may still be annoyed, but at least, they are the ones who allowed you to make them wait. Unless you deal in emergency situations, clients should be able to leave a message, and expect a quick call back. If you do not provide the <u>call back within 5 to 15 minutes</u>, expect that clients will keep calling and paging you all the time.

Another thing that happens quite often is that Service reps transfer clients to other staff members without verifying if someone will answer. <u>Never transfer to an empty phone</u>. If a client is being transferred, their happiness level is already injured, so imagine if they go straight to the other person's voicemail. As a Service rep you should always confirm that the other employee is available and aware of what is coming. By providing the employee the back-story you prevent them from being blind-sighted, and it prevents the client from having to repeat their story. If the person is unavailable, ask the client if they prefer to wait, go to voicemail, or see if there is anything else you can do.

CAN YOU SEE ME SMILE... OVER THE PHONE?

At times, this will be your most arduous task... Day in day out, whatever is happening around you or in your private life, you must be joyful and enthusiastic. This is apparent of course if you deal with clients face-to-face. But phone reps must also do this. As ridiculous as it sounds, the person at the other end of the receiver will feel you smile when you talk to them and will act accordingly. Even you will notice that most grumpy people become more upbeat once you talk to them using this principle. The idea here is that you must make the person at the other end feel like you are happy to talk to them. That will put them at ease and will make the icy-est client melt...

I would have loved to include an example of this theme for you however it is not possible to do it justice in written format. All I can really add to what I have said so far would be to physically smile while on the phone, and to be positive and upbeat. Sometimes it might help to remember a situation when you were very happy (calling your friends to tell them you won a contest, etc.)

I have personally been known to apply this theme to the extreme... Clients calling me will usually be welcomed by a larger than life character called Frrrrancesco. The creation of an alter-ego has allowed me to keep my spirits up no matter what happens. Of course, I tone it down when a problem arises so to make the client understand how concerned I am. The worse thing you could do would be to make the client feel like you are making fun or are not serious about the issue at hand. The alter-ego is a trick you can try.

YOUR WORD IS GOLDEN

Trust is key to a successful relationship. If you say you will do something, do it. If you tell a client you will call them within 15 minutes, make sure you know when that is, and make sure you call them within that time frame. <u>You must develop a trust with the client</u>. The more they trust you, the less they will harass you, the happier they will be. Clients who do not trust you will make your life miserable and will always be stressed when dealing with you. The ideal situation is where the client is calm and confident about your ability to complete a task or achieve a result.

SMALL TALK

Engaging in small talk is encouraged but there must be boundaries. You can talk about the weather, their children, but you must steer the conversation so you are not on the phone with the same person for too long. The purpose of small talk is to get what you need, and to enhance or deepen your relationship with the client (for the company). You are not there to make lasting friends, but business partners. Steering the conversation toward hanging up is sometimes delicate. You must find a way to get off the phone without offending your contact. Here are a few examples that may help. Note that your choice has to be made based on the strength of your relationship with the client; the more you know them, the more latitude you will have:

- I have taken enough of your time, thank you for everything... or
- I'd love to chat but I want to make sure I get through your file...or
- Alright, I'll let you go back to work now...or
- I have another line. They're not as important as you of course but...or
- I have a nice person standing right next to me with a big stack of documents, I think I should let you go...

Example of "Small Talk"

> CLIENT: Hello John!
>
> Response
>
> Well hello Steve! Long time no speak! How are you?
>
> CLIENT: I'm OK, you?
>
> Response
>
> I am excellent thank you! How's the little one?... His name is Max, right?
>
> CLIENT: He's great! He just started to walk last week... Remind me, do you have any kids?
>
> Response
>
> Not yet! I am still waiting for the right woman... So what gives me the pleasure of speaking with you on this beautiful day?
>
> CLIENT: I just wanted to see when my order would be delivered!
>
> Response
>
> I checked a few moments ago and delivery is estimated for tomorrow in the afternoon. Just let me know by then if there is a problem!
>
> CLIENT: Thanks. Any plans for the week-end?
>
> Response
>
> Nothing much... Probably yard work!
>
> CLIENT: Fun stuff I see... I think we're going to see that new movie coming out!
>
> Response
>
> Lucky guy...! Oh-oh, I have an accounting lady here looking at me funny... I think I might be in trouble... You have a great week-end and send me a quick email when you get your delivery just so I can sleep better on the week-end!
>
> CLIENT: No problem... And good luck!

COULD CLIENTS BE ST*P*D?

You must smile and laugh with a client, but never laugh AT a client... Remember that there are no stupid questions...

Example of "Could Clients be..."

> CLIENT: At what time does the 4 O'clock train arrive?
>
> BAD Response
>
> At 4, of course...!
>
> BETTER Response
>
> This train usually arrives around 4 [NO SARCASM PLEASE].

Usually the client will realize that their question was quite dimwitted but you must reassure them. Tell them this happens all the time and not to worry about it.

CONCLUSION

I hope you have been able to find enough information and examples here to fit your business, yourself, and your company. As I said in the introduction, the purpose of this book was to provide the philosophy and the tools to help you dispense great Customer Service. With time and practice, Servicing will become second nature and you will find yourself doing it well without trying. The downside is that you will easily pinpoint the failings of all the people servicing you, from the donut shop to the civil servant...

Good Luck!

MANAGERS! SUPPORT YOUR EMPLOYEES

After reading this guide, taking notes, and discussing the concepts among yourselves and with your superiors, your task is to make sure your employees are well-acquainted with what is needed to provide great Customer Service. As much as you might be asked to keep track of results and tendencies, your primary role is to support your staff so they can follow this guide and give your company high levels of satisfaction and client retention. Here are a few concepts designed specifically for you.

Some companies have music or have a script running when clients are placed on hold. I often hear things like "your call is important to us...". My suggestion here would be to change this line to "<u>YOU are important to us</u>...". This is a much more powerful phrase and has a better chance of making the person waiting on the line, feel validated, and less prone to scream when your staff picks up the line.

A manager/supervisor should be someone <u>who leads by example</u>. Someone who knows the principles of this book, and more importantly, who applies them when he/she is in contact with clients. You should <u>always be calm</u> (to avoid stressing out employees), yet <u>understand urgency and be able to prioritize</u>. You should be someone people aspire to become, and who <u>respects employees</u> and the work they do. You should be a <u>good teacher</u>, coaching the staff and assisting them when they have difficult calls, or when they are unsure how to respond to certain situations.

Making sure your department is efficient is your job, not the employees'. Their job is to be effective, to provide the best

Customer Service they can, while you have to work on finding the best (and cheapest) way to <u>support their efforts</u>.

If a service failure occurred and an employee comes to you with the client's complaint asking how they should resolve the issue, give yourself some time to think about it and discuss it with colleagues (if need be). Then explain to your Service personnel what the answer is, why this is, how you came about to this solution, and suggest alternate ways to convey the information to the client.

Depending on your business, you may <u>place your employees in charge of a group of customers</u>. The grouping can be done based on geography, volume, or even alphabet, and this will give them a sense of ownership. Clients will no longer be anonymous, and employees will no longer be just another phone attendant. They will be able to develop relationships and help the company grow stronger.

A manager should also be able to <u>empower the employees</u> to make decisions once they have proven themselves. This could mean allowing them to give clients limited refunds or gratuities. You could even provide a pool of these for them to use, and tie it to their next salary review. A certain degree of empowerment will prevent employees from having to come back to you with requests and make the client wait for the answer. It further helps in developing the relationship.

CASE STUDY I: Cable Installation

SITUATION:

I work for a cable company. A client has been waiting all day but the installation crew mis-managed their time and will not be able to do the installation for this client.

WHAT I HAVE DONE:

I have explained to the dispatcher how unacceptable this was, and appealed with her to see if the crew could go later; they could not. This means that the client will have to wait another day. I was able to make the dispatcher promise that the client would be first on the list, whatever day they would be available, including tomorrow.

SCRIPT:

- Unfortunately the installation cannot be done today.

- Why? Delayed by several longer installations in the morning.

- Why only calling in the afternoon? They did everything possible to catch up, but realized they could not make it.

- Can they come tonight? Unfortunately I verified with dispatcher and they have other late installations

- I know it's inconvenient but when can they go next? **Promise to be first on the list** They start at 8:00

- Compensation? (manager says I can't give anything)

ACTUAL CALL:

Rep> Mr. Johnson, this is Larry from Cable Co.. I know you've been waiting all day but our installation crew just advised me that they will unfortunately not be able to come today!

Client> What do you mean?

Rep> They were delayed at several other sites earlier today. They tried their best to catch up, but they just realized that they would not be able to come today. I understand this is really inconvenient for you but I was able to make them promise that you would be the first on the list, whatever weekday you would be available!

Client> This is a real problem. I have to stay home from work waiting for you guys...

Rep> I know... And will remind the dispatcher... But they had a few problematic installations and they really tried to catch up... We could come tomorrow morning at about 8:00.

Client> Alright that's fine... But are you going to compensate me for this?

Rep> Unfortunately, as I mentioned before, the delay is really not something they could have planned for and they really did all they could to make the appointment. But what I will do is call you tomorrow at around 8:30 to make sure they came by, and please don't hesitate to call me if you have any questions. My name is Larry and you can reach me at our 1.800 number, my extension is 1844. Again I am sorry about the inconvenience and I will speak to you again tomorrow around 8:30.

Client> OK

Rep> Thank you.

AFTERMATH:

I immediately called the Dispatcher to schedule the installation, reminding her of the promise she made, and confirmed twice that the crew will be there at 8:00 the next morning. I called the client at 8:30 the day of, and the crew had not arrived. I placed the client on hold (with his permission) while I contacted the dispatcher. She said the crew had just arrived. I went back on the line with the client and he confirmed they were there, and then he thanked me for everything...

CASE STUDY II: Broken Delivery

SITUATION:

I am a driver for a popular courier company. One day I had a package for Irene Goldstein. As soon as I took the box out of my truck I heard broken glass...

WHAT I HAVE DONE:

I could have made the decision of returning the box back to my office, make a report and potentially have the box returned to the shipper, but I figured that either I was wrong and nothing was broken, or that perhaps only some of the contents were broken. I could have also played dumb and not say a word... But I decided to deliver the item and alert the client to my suspicions.

SCRIPT:

- Hello...

- Seems like there might be some damage

- Open it in front of me?

ACTUAL EVENT:

Driver> Hello! I am looking for Miss or Mrs Irene Goldstein!

Client> I am Miss Goldstein!

Driver> I have this package for you!

Client> Oh wonderful... I have been waiting days for this...!

Driver> Here it is! I have to warn you though... [I shook the box delicately until she heard the noise]

Driver> ... I am not sure if it's supposed to do that!

Client> Oh... Not at all...!

Driver> Do you want to open the package while I am here so I can immediately make a report if there are any damages?

Client> Please!

I pulled my utility knife and handed it to her (handle first) then placed the box on the floor. She cut the tape and pulled the flaps open. Right away I saw bubble wrap everywhere. She pulled out one item and took it out of the packaging. The vase looked perfect. She pulled the second vase and it also looked unscathed. But as she lifted the third item we saw some glass at the bottom.

Driver> I am sorry about this Miss Goldstein. I don't know where or how the vase was broken, but as soon as I return to my office I will have them put notes in the system explaining that out of 3 well-protected vases, one was broken. I know it's inconvenient, but if you call the person who shipped this to you (I pointed to the shipper on the label and their phone number) they can surely file an insurance claim and send you a new one! I am really sorry about all this but I hope you can still have a good day...!

I gave her a little smile, she responded in kind, and I returned to my route. As soon as I came back to my office I advised the floor supervisor about the incident and he put notes in the system. I then took the tracking number, the name of the client, her address, and today's date so I could follow up.

AFTERMATH:

Two days later I used one of our terminals before my shift to see if there was an update. The system showed that the shipper had issued a claim and that the value of the vase was $60. Knowing that my company automatically reimburses up to

$100, the shipper would get a full refund. That same day I had a light run so I stopped by Miss Goldstein's residence.

Client> Oh... Hello young man!

Driver> Hello Miss Goldstein! How are you today?

Client> Very well thank you... I called the company, like you said, and they are shipping me a new vase!

Driver> Excellent! I am very happy for you!

Client> Thank you very much!

Driver> Very well... I will see you again soon then...

It so happens that the very next day I delivered the replacement vase to Miss Goldstein. She was very excited and I asked again if she could open the box while I was there just so I was sure that everything was OK... and it was.

Client> You know, my grandson keeps complaining about his delivery company... You were very good, maybe he should use you!

Driver> He should... Would you like to give me the name of his company?

She quickly pulled out his business card. As soon as I returned to my office I went to see one of our salespeople, told him the story of the broken vase and gave him the business card.

CASE STUDY III: Lawn Contract

SITUATION:

During summer and between semesters I cut grass for a landscaping company. Mr. Greene was a new client with a very nice front yard. It was not enormous but it took me about 30 minutes to get the job done. As I was packing up my equipment into the truck, Mr. Green came out of his house waving his arms... "Hey! Where are you going? You didn't do the backyard yet!" I was surprised since my work order only showed that I had to do the front lawn...

SCRIPT:

The client was right in front of me so there was no time to make a script...

ACTUAL EVENT:

Employee> Hello Sir! Maybe this is just a misprint on my work order. Let me call my manager, it will only take a minute!

I climbed into the cab of my truck and called my manager using my cell phone.

Employee> Hello, Jim? I'm at the Greene residence and the client believes I should also mow his backyard but my papers show I am only supposed to do the front...!

Manager> No... The paper's right. I'm the one who did the contract. He only signed up for the front yard. Just remind him about it and go to your next site!

I got out of the truck and went to see the client.

Client> So?

Employee> My manager just advised me that he reviewed your file and that you had contracted us only to do the front yard...!

Client> What? That's just stupid. Why would I do that?

Employee> You are obviously upset and this is probably just a misunderstanding. I don't like to do this but I do have to go... What I will do though is ask if you can pull your service contract during the day and I will ask Jim, my manager to call you later on to confirm. And if there is a misunderstanding I will make sure to come back and do your backyard tomorrow, weather permitting...!

I called Jim after I left and told him what I had promised the client.

AFTERMATH:

The next day, I called Jim after finishing my first job to make sure he had called Mr. Greene. I was happy I did because he had completely forgotten. I also asked him to call me back when he had made the call so I knew what had happened.

Manager> Okay, I just spoke to the client. He saw that the contract was only for the front yard but he says that it was not clear when he agreed to give us the job. I told him I would have you do the backyard some time this week and we would adjust the pricing agreement. Since this seems like an honest misunderstanding I gave him a discount. So I will put him on your schedule by Friday!

Employee> Excellent. I actually started earlier today in case I would have to go back. So if you don't mind, I will go see him after lunch!

Manager> Good thinking. Let me know how it goes!

I got to Mr. Greene's house after lunch and rang the doorbell.

Client> Already?

Employee> I did promise you to come back today if things cleared up!

Client> That's very good... You know, I'm still not ecstatic about this whole thing, but you're a good kid!

Employee> Thank you. We do what we can. Is there anything you want to mention about the backyard or should I just do like I did in the front?

Client> Just be careful around the pool, but apart from that nothing special!

CASE STUDY IV: Screaming for a Phone

SITUATION:

I manage my company's main downtown branch. We sell mobile phones, related services, and we are the only center doing repairs and replacements. While serving a customer I had caught a potential situation developing at the service counter with the corner of my eye. A man was speaking loudly and waving his limbs around. The attendant seemed to deal with the sitation and did not look over at me for assistance. All of a sudden, the man started yelling obscenities at my employee.

WHAT I HAVE DONE:

I politely asked my client to excuse me as I pointed to the overactive man. He seemed to understand as I promised him I would send someone to help him.

SCRIPT:

I had no idea what the situation was so I really could not prepare...

ACTUAL EVENT:

Manager> Hello! My name is John and I am the manager here!

Client> Well your F***ing employee here won't help me!

Manager> I am sorry sir. I see you are upset but there is no need for this kind of language. Now let's see if I can help you!

I turned to my employee...

Manager> Mike, could you go see this client (the one I had just abandoned), He wants a phone with access to emails but he has a couple of questions... Thank you!

Usually I would have preferred to have Mike with me so the irate client would not have to repeat his story, but the man seemed much too upset...

Manager> So how can I help sir!

Client> I just got this phone and it doesn't work! You need to give me a new one!

Mike had already opened the phone. I immediately knew just by looking at it that the phone had been dropped in water. But I played the game anyway. I asked the client his name and reviewed his file on our system.

Manager> The circuits look corroded. Almost like the phone was dropped in water...

Client> Well it wasn't!

Manager> I see in our system that you got this phone two months ago?

Client> I don't remember!

Manager> And at that time it was a replacement for a phone that was also defective!

Client> Ya, so!

Manager> Let me take it to the back and have a specialist look at it!

I was pretty sure this client was finding new and interesting ways of upgrading his phone, but I just wanted to make sure.

Specialist> Woah... That phone went swimmin'?

Manager> I thought so too... In your experience is there any possibility that this could be a manufacturing defect.

Specialist> Only if they manufactured it under water...!

Manager> Sir, unfortunately my specialist and I believe that this damage could not be a manufacturing defect, and since you already had the phone for a few weeks, it is much more likely that someone may have dropped your phone in water and did not tell you...!

Client> What the F**k! Are you calling me a liar?

Manager> Not at all sir. These things happen... A friend or a child may have taken your phone without your knowledge and they may have been too ashamed or afraid to tell you what happened.

Client> You're an a****le!

Manager> I am sorry sir. I know you are upset but there is no need for this kind of language. Unfortunately I will not be able to exchange your phone but I see that you have accumulated points and you could use them against the purchase of a new phone!

Client> You people s**k! You know what? This is not worth it! You don't want my business, I'll take it elsewhere!

Manager> I understand your frustration and you ARE an important client. We simply cannot exchange this phone. It might be more expensive in the long run to go somewhere else... But if you are really sure, I could cancel your account now and we could calculate the cancellation fees together. But I strongly suggest you review your options. I would be more than happy to do it with you, or you can review some of our information online or by calling our toll-free number!

The client took back his phone and left the store...

AFTERMATH:

I went back to see the client I had left to deal with this situation. He was at the cash with Mike, signing his new contract.

Manager> So... Did Mike take good care of you?

Client> Very well!

Manager> I am not surprised. He's one of my top guys! Which phone did you get?

Client> I got this new Blackberry... Mike says it's the best!

Once the transaction was over and the customer left the store, I took Mike aside.

Mike> This guy was insane wasn't he?

Manager> I think he was just upset that we wouldn't give him a new phone. What happened before I got there?

Mike> He gave me his phone. I opened it and I saw right away that he had dropped it in water. I told him I couldn't exchange it. He started screaming at me.!

Manager> Ya... He was pretty aggressive!

I then proceeded to tell Mike how I handled the situation never making him feel like I was better. I just recounted the facts.

Manager> ...And thank you for taking care of my client... You did a really good job!

ABOUT THE AUTHOR

After graduating McGill University, Francesco Messina started his career with one of Canada's most important textile-based Customs brokerage firms. He instantly began impressing his managers and clients with his seemingly innate brand of Customer satisfaction. Soon, he was asked to teach and manage others, leading him to create the company's standard for delivering Customer Service which is still being taught today. He blames his own demanding personality for being able to serve every client beyond their expectations. Francesco currently works as a manager for the third largest global distributor of electronic components in the world.

"Our clients speak very highly of him, as a problem solver, and someone they know will take their issue at heart and treat them like he would if he was in their shoes".

-Ross James, President, Omnitrans Pacific.

"[...] will certainly miss working with you as you've made our relationship [...] one of the best in our client portfolio."

-Michael Trueman, Executive Vice President, Go-Logix Technologies.

"Francesco... It's becoming "tiresome" having all these clients calling and sending faxes on how amazing a job you're doing![...]"

-Stephen Segal, Vice President, Omnitans Inc.

"In laymen's words... "HE'S REALLY GOOD".

-Richard Rubin, President, Agritrade International.